T0099748

THE
EMPERORS
NO
CLOTHES

THE
EMPERORS
NO
CLOTHES

John Taylor

BALBOA.
PRESS

A DIVISION OF HAY HOUSE

Balboa Press books may be ordered through booksellers or by contacting:

Balboa Press
A Division of Hay House
1663 Liberty Drive
Bloomington, IN 47403
www.balboapress.com.au
1-(877) 407-4847

ISBN: 978-1-4525-0562-6 (sc)
ISBN: 978-1-4525-0563-3 (e)

Because of the dynamic nature of the Internet, any web addresses or
links contained in this book may have changed since publication and
may no longer be valid. The views expressed in this work are solely those
of the author and do not necessarily reflect the views of the publisher,
and the publisher hereby disclaims any responsibility for them.

The author of this book does not dispense medical advice or prescribe the use
of any technique as a form of treatment for physical, emotional, or medical
problems without the advice of a physician, either directly or indirectly.   The
intent of the author is only to offer information of a general nature to help you
in your quest for emotional and spiritual well-being. In the event you use
any of the information in this book for yourself, which is your constitutional
right, the author and the publisher assume no responsibility for your actions.

Any people depicted in stock imagery provided by Thinkstock are models,
and such images are being used for illustrative purposes only.
Certain stock imagery © Thinkstock.

Printed in the United States of America

Balboa Press rev. date: 06/26/2012

TABLE OF CONTENTS

CHAPTER 1

THE NEW CLOTHES

You have probably heard the Hans Christian Andersen Fairy Tale about the Emperor and his new clothes. It's a great little story and I love the song Danny Kaye sings "The King is in His altogether He's altogether as naked as the day that he was born". This is how the story goes.

Many years ago, there lived an Emperor who was so fond of new clothes that he spent all his money on them in order to be beautifully dressed. He did not care about his soldiers, he did not care about the theatre; he only liked to go out walking to show off his new clothes. He had a coat for every hour of the day and, just as they say of a king, "He is in the council-chamber," they always said here, "The Emperor is in the wardrobe."

In the great city in which he lived, there was always something going on. Every day, many strangers came there. One day, two impostors arrived who claimed to be weavers and said that they knew how to manufacture the most beautiful cloth imaginable. Not only were the texture and pattern uncommonly beautiful, but the clothes which were made of this material possessed the wonderful property that they were invisible to anyone who was not fit for his office, or who was unpardonably stupid.

"Those must indeed be splendid clothes," thought the Emperor. "If I had them on, I could find out which men in my kingdom are unfit for the offices they hold. I could distinguish the wise from the stupid! Yes, this cloth must be woven for me at once." And he gave both the impostors much money so that they might begin their work.

He sent his most trusted ministers and court officials to check out the new clothes being made. Of course they saw nothing but, not wanting to appear stupid, they fell in with the con. All the ministers, not wanting to appear stupid, approved. They are truly beautiful, agreed the court officials. "Oh, it is lovely, most lovely," they said. 'What a texture! What colours! Yes, we will tell the Emperor that it pleases us very much."

So off went the Emperor, parading through the streets with his new clothes. Of course his subjects, not wanting to appear stupid either, cheered approval. "What beautiful clothes," they exclaimed.

AND THEN IT HAPPENED
THE NO CLOTHES

"But he has nothing on!" said a little child at last.

"Just listen to the innocent child!" said the father, and each one whispered to his neighbour what the child had said.

"But he has nothing on," the whole of the people called out at last.

This struck the Emperor, for it seemed to him as if they were right; but he thought to himself, "I must go on with the procession now," and the chamberlains walked along still more uprightly, holding up the train which was not there at all.

Hans Christian Anderson "The Emperors new clothes"

Now this is a Fairy Tale, a children's story. Nobody really believes it.

Or do we? . . . . You might be surprised.

We have actually invented a King with no clothes, and, not wanting to appear stupid; millions of people believe that this King and his clothes are real. There is a very sinister reason for getting people to believe that this King and his clothes are real but we will get to that later.

where did he come from?

Before we start to put some respectable clothes on this King, let's first look at the King himself and find out where he came from.

As it turns out, this guy just simply appeared from nowhere and apparently from nothing. He had absolutely no form. He came from nothing. But everybody knows that you can't get something coming from nothing so we had to give this nothing a name. We called it "Spontaneous Generation" leading to the King that we now call evolution.

What in the world is "Spontaneous Generation"? Good question!

According to Wikipedia, the theory of Spontaneous Generation held that "complex living organisms may be produced from nonliving matter" It was a popular belief, for years, that mice occur spontaneously from stored grain and maggots spontaneously appear in meat.

The main problem with this theory is that it there is no evidence of it ever happening. In fact, it has been totally disproved.

A committed evolutionist, Dr. George Wald who won the Nobel Prize for physiology in 1967 and professor emeritus of biology at Harvard University, has this to say about it:

"There are two possible explanations as to how life arose: Spontaneous Generation arising to evolution, or a Supernatural creative act of God . . . There are no other possibilities. Spontaneous generation was scientifically disproved 120 years ago by Louis Pasteur and others. That just leaves us with only one other possibility . . . that life came as a supernatural act of creation by God.

But I can't accept that philosophy (says Dr. Wald) because I do not want to believe in God. Therefore, I choose to believe in that which I know is scientifically impossible: Spontaneous Generation leading to evolution."

Scientific Creationism Vs Evolution—Spontaneous Generation (The Origin of Life," Scientific American, Vol. 190, pp. 46-50)

With credentials and a reference like that, this King hasn't got too much going for him, has he?

But that's OK. Let's not get too pedantic. Let's not let a little impossibility get in the way of a ridiculous story. After all, if we let facts stop us, we would never get this King started.

Now that we have him well and truly established as a result of Spontaneous Generation,(which is impossible) we need to start putting some clothes on him. We can't have a King running about the place naked, can we?

The problem is, no matter how hard we try to put clothes on this poor bloke, we can't seem to get anything to fit.

CHAPTER 2

THE EMPERORS CHAMPION

This Emperor really needs a champion to help him.

On the scene came a genius named **★Charles Darwin**, and all the people rejoiced and were glad, for a savior had come to clothe the Emperor.

And behold, the savior proclaimed the "<u>Theory of Evolution</u>" as the Emperor's new clothes made from the cloth of "Natural Selection" stitched together with" Missing links".

If you don't know what a missing link is, don't be too concerned; neither does anybody else. Once again, we won't let that stop the wheels of progress. The King still needs some clothes so we continue to dress him in these beautiful clothes even though they are completely and totally invisible.

*Charles Darwin (1809-1882)** was born into a wealthy family. He dropped out of medical school at Edinburgh University after only two years. This apparently was the only scientific training he ever had. However, Darwin also studied Theology at Cambridge University. The teaching at that time claimed that the book of Genesis taught that no variation could occur in nature which meant that all species were an exact replica of their ancestors.

When Darwin set off on his five year voyage around the world on the Beagle, he presumed that if the Genesis account was true, he could expect to see species that had been created, placed in their environment and remain unchanged.

What he did find however caused him concern. Instead of finding evidence that the basic types had been created and placed where he found them, he found many species which appeared to have migrated from other parts of the earth and adapted to suit their new environment.

On nine of the largest islands of the Galapagos, Darwin found among other species, fourteen different species of giant land tortoises the genera for these Tortoises were found to be the same as the species found in South and Central America. The fact was that all of them were still giant land tortoises which had developed variations within the species known as Micro evolution. Darwin presumed this to be evidence of Macro evolution (changing from one species to a different species)

There was evidence of variation all over the place but he never saw any evidence whatsoever of the origin of new basic types. Darwin believed that the book of Genesis taught no variation. He saw that all the species he encountered, repeatedly came from basic types, but his failure to recognize this very important fact, gave rise to the inspiration for his book, "Origin of Species"

Origin of the Species, was first published in November 1859. In it Darwin often cited authorities that he did not mention. When he did name an authority, it was generally only an opinion and words like, "Maybe", "probably," "it is conceivable that" are mentioned regularly in the book. A favorite of his was: "Let us take an imaginary example" Remember the words in the fairy tale? "The new clothes were invisible to anyone who was not fit for his office, or who was unpardonably stupid". Do they sound a wee bit similar? I hear the same thing today over TV, radio, written in newspapers and magazines. Commentators are continually suggesting that There is overwhelming evidence for evolution but nobody ever comes up with such evidence. Why this theory was accepted so eagerly by so many people, is a complete mystery, but it was. I have heard it said that if you tell a lie often enough and loud enough people will believe it. At that time, there was a movement to find something different. It did not have to be true; it just had to be different, a little bit sensational. That started the ball rolling. No evidence, no facts, just different.

Many years ago, I was a police officer in Scotland. Part of the duties of the police, were to appear in court and give evidence, usually against someone who had allegedly broken the law. Can you imagine what the judge would have said if I had stood in the court and said "there is overwhelming evidence that the accused assaulted his wife, and then could not produce the evidence? I won't even answer that question because no police officer who wanted to keep his job would have dreamed of saying something so stupid. And yet we get the devotees of evolution spouting it continually. Even more unbelievable is that thousands of people believe it.

I was watching a show on TV last night it's called "Unforgettable" and I just had to write the dialogue down as it went along. The accused was charged with murder but the witness for the prosecution did not turn up at the trial. Some documents that were critical to the case were also missing. The judge then asked the prosecutor, "Do you have any further evidence that you can present to the court? The Prosecutor said "no your Honour" The judge then said "I have no option, therefore, than to dismiss this case. "CASE DISMISSED". No witness, no evidence, case dismissed. Do I need to say more?

Darwin often said that his book was an abstract which would be followed at a later date with a more complete version of the theory but that simply has never happened, neither Darwin nor anybody else has ever been able to find proof or even credible evidence for the evolution theory. He often suggested that something could have occurred, and then referred back to it as a fact: He extrapolated that there must have been a time when species must 'have been changing in other parts of the world where the strata had not yet been examined.

These changed species then somehow reached the Western World, and were discovered in strata there as new species. And that is why we don't find the changes into other species together. With thinking like this, who needs science or evidence?

"Origin of Species" is not too often referred by the scientific fraternity today because there is simply no scientific evidence for the theory it suggests. Darwin taught that we had all originated from a common ancestor, eventually apes turned into men and that the stronger races would overtake the weaker ones.

If this were the case, surely we would have been physically stronger and more agile than apes but we are not

He frequently commented in private letters that he recognized that there was no evidence for his theory, and that it could destroy the morality of the human race.

So that's the story of Darwin. The following is an explanation of the "<u>Theory Of Evolution</u>".

CHAPTER 3

THE THEORY

The Theory of Evolution claims that all life comes from the one source, for example, all animals, plants and every other life form came from the same ancestor. This, according to the geniuses of evolution, all started with spontaneous generation, followed by natural selection and Lamarckism (the inheritance of acquired characteristics); these are the basis of biological evolution yet, all of these theories have been disproven by scientists. But hang on a minute, if the first part of the theory, that life started from nothing and came about by spontaneous generation, has since been proved to be impossible, why would you go on to even talk about evolution through natural selection? If you can't get the thing started in the first place, the rest of it is purely academic. It's a bit like building a submarine with holes in it and then planning what route you will take to sail it from England to France. This is just plain stupid, if the thing doesn't work to start with, it's not going anywhere.

This King we have invented doesn't really exist. There is no evidence for his existence. He is nothing more than a figment of an overly active imagination for the purpose of getting rid of God. When that is your primary goal you don't need facts or evidence you just need to tell the lie often enough and loud enough and eventually people start to believe it. Remember what George Wald said. "There are only two ways we could have got here". Using your experience and intelligence, you need to decide, based on the evidence available, which one makes sense Spontaneous generation or Creation?

But there we go again, using logic and common sense, we need to stop doing this if we want to have an Emperor and have nice clothes for him to wear, and so it goes on.

The evolutionary worldview is not a recent theory. The development of life from non-life and the evolutionary descent of man from animals were suggested by many of the ancient philosophers. When Charles Darwin came up with the idea of natural selection, it brought something new to the old philosophy. A reasonable explanation for the old idea had been found. Now the theory that life somehow got started from non-life and that complex creatures evolved from more simplistic ancestors naturally over time became more acceptable.

The theory then suggests, that as genetic mutations randomly evolved, the favorable mutations were maintained because they aided survival. These favorable mutations were then inherited by the following generation. For example, if a species developed something that would be an advantage, such as sprouting wings and was able to fly, it's descendants would inherit that advantage and pass it on to their descendants. The inferior (disadvantaged) members of the same species would gradually die out, leaving only the superior (advantaged) members of the species. Eventually these favorable mutations accumulate and turn into an entirely different species. This new idea took on a new life and blossomed into the mess we have today.

This creates a bit of a problem for creatures like the woodpecker. This busy little creature has the habit using its bill for drumming and hammering on trees. The evolution theorists suggest that woodpeckers have evolved a number of adaptations similar to a sponge like shock absorber. This protects the brain and prevents brain damage from the rapid and repeated knocking.

The problem is what happened before these adaptations evolved? I can just imagine every time the woodpeckers' bill hits the tree, its bill would come shooting through the back of its head. Now that would severely damage the process of evolution. The protection needs to be there at the very beginning. That is not evolution, that's creation.

Slowly, but surely . . .

According to Darwin, the theory of evolution is a slow, gradual process. Natural selection can only come about gradually by small progressive steps. It cannot suddenly change from one species to another. That's the theory, but once again, we run into some more problems. This is what Darwin had to say about his own theory.

Darwin commented in his book known as Origin of Species "If it could be demonstrated that any complex organ existed, which could not possibly have been formed by numerous, successive, slight modifications, my theory would absolutely break down".

Charles Darwin, "On the Origin of Species by Means of Natural Selection, or the Preservation of Favoured Races in the Struggle for Life," 1859, p.162.

But then Niles Eldredge and Stephen Jay Gould both committed evolutionists have disputed the original Darwinian theory and suggested that evolution tends to happen in fits and starts, sometimes moving very fast, sometimes moving very slowly or sometimes not at all. This was in total disagreement with Darwin.

They called this "punctuated equilibrium"

Darwin says he thinks it happened slowly. Eldredge and Gould say it either happened fast or slow or sometime not at all but none of them can come up with a scrap of evidence as to exactly when it happened, where it happened, how it happened and what it happened to. But that doesn't matter you only need to believe without question or evidence, that it did happen. Now that takes faith, an awful lot of faith.

This crazy theory just keeps coming up with one problem after another. Let's have a look at the incredibly complex system like your eye, if you stop to think about it, it's quite fascinating. Whether you stop to think about it or not, it's still quite fascinating.

I am in no way going to attempt to fit all the details of how the eye works into this little story, it is much too complicated for that, but just to give you an overview of some of the remarkable things your eye is doing as you are reading this book. Here is a very small outline of how it works.

The human eye adapts to changing lighting conditions and distances. Try it, move close to this page and then move back a little bit, you can still read it because the eye adjusts to consider the distance.

Now walk from a light room to a darker room, at first you can't see a thing, but your eyes gradually adjust to the conditions and soon you can make out various objects in the darker room.

Think of your eye as a very sophisticated camera:

The cornea is like a lens cover. As the eye's main focusing element, the cornea takes widely diverging rays of light and bends them through the pupil.

The pupil, is the dark, round opening in the centre of the coloured iris.

The iris and pupil act like the aperture of a camera. Then you've got the lens

The lens acts like the lens in a camera, helping to focus light to the back of the eye. Then there's the retina.

The retina is a membrane containing photoreceptor nerve cells that lines the inside back wall of the eye

The photoreceptor nerve cells of the retina change the light rays into electrical impulses.

The optic nerve sends these electrical impulses through to the brain where an image is perceived.

Another two things we need to be aware of, the first one is that each of us has two of these things, and secondly, we need big holes in our skull to fit them into.

Now here's the thing, Your eye adapts to changing light and distances, it has a cornea, a pupil, an iris, a lens, a retina, photoreceptor nerve cells, an optic nerve, and to make it all work together you need to have a structure which links the whole system up to the brain. We're not even going to think about the brain, that's just too much to deal with here.

Now here's the question, Have you ever in all of your life seen, heard of, or even imagined all those linked things coming about slowly and gradually one after the other by accident? We need a yes/no answer here.

Of course you haven't it's just too ridiculous. Every single part has to be there at the same time for any of the parts to function, otherwise nothing works.

Then, of course, we have these little doors at the front of our eyes, we call them eyelids, they are really quite fascinating. Your brain can send a message to these little doors and tell them to blink and in a split second they close and open. You can send the message to wink and one eye shuts and opens, I do not suggest that you use this function when looking at the opposite sex; you could get in a bit of trouble or end up with a partner for the rest of your life. You can close both of the doors of your eyes at the same time to keep light out and open them to let light in. The mechanics involved in these procedures is far beyond my understanding but I am totally convinced that they did not happen through undirected chance or accident. If these things did happen by accident: when did they happen? How did they happen?

We are told that such complicated systems like the eyes and the eyelids somehow managed to evolve gradually without direction or supervision (excuse the pun) and yet we cannot imagine a manmade product or system just happening by chance.

Here is one small example:

When I get to about 10-12 metres away from home, I press a button on a device which I attached to the steering wheel of my car and the roller door of my garage opens. When I get inside the garage, I press the same little button and the door closes. Now if I told you that, over a period of time, the roller door gradually grew into a space at the entrance to the garage and over a period of time started to recognize my car and automatically opened by itself when the car approached and then automatically closed by itself when the car was inside: you would probably think I was living in fantasy land. The first question you would need to ask is: how did the garage door get there in the first place? The second question is, why does it respond to the little device on the steering wheel of my car?

Now I know nothing about electronics but I have enough intelligence and experience to work out that the logical conclusion would be that someone put that garage door there and then designed the little device with the button so that it would send a message to the garage door and something would work out whether it needed to open or close, and the door would respond accordingly.

Now that makes sense but we are asked to believe, that every time you open or close your eyes, blink or wink, that your ability to do this came about by an accidental process of evolution over an unknown period of time.

I think we are back to fantasy land again.

To make the eye and all the other systems throughout the body work, it is absolutely essential that all the working parts need to be in place at the same time. The cornea, pupil, Iris and lens of the eye are useless individually; the whole system depends on each one playing its part before any of them can work. This system is now recognized as, "irreducible complexity". Our entire body is made up of irreducible complex parts.

Michael Behe wrote about it in his book "Darwins Black Box"

Referring to the living cell, Michael Behe states:

Such a system could not have evolved slowly, piece by piece. In order for a living cell to operate, it would require all parts of the system to be present at the same time. This is known as "irreducible complexity". The incredible complex living cell is also irreducibly complex, it is impossible for it to operate without every single part being present right from the start.

Michael Behe, "The Black Box," 1996

Michael Denton had this to say about it:

We don't need a microscope to observe irreducible complexity. The eye, the ear and the heart are all examples of irreducible complexity, though they were not recognized as such in Darwin's day

Michael Denton, "Evolution: A Theory in Crisis," 1986, p. 250

But, now that we have got the whole thing started through Spontaneous Generation, let's ignore the fact that it cannot happen, the previous information about your eye, the quotations from Darwin, Denton and Behe, and go into the mechanics of the evolutionary theory. You see, we need to convince the general public that the King and his invisible clothes are real but up until now we are not doing too well.

To keep this charade going we need to come up with something that will keep the public interest alive, something a bit sensational. People love sensational stuff. To do this, the idea that human beings came from monkeys is employed, we are not quite sure what kind of monkeys we came from, but who cares, any kind of monkey will do for the purpose of getting us to believe this nonexistent King and his invisible clothes are real. So the evolutionists come up with the story that once upon a time (I think that's a lovely way to start a story) there was half-man, half-ape creatures walking about the earth. Fantastic, and when people realize that the evidence that has been presented to support this story is a load of nonsense, they will come up with another one. They can keep this going for years.

Now that's a great idea but the problem is what evidence do we put forward to support it? Well that's not all that difficult to do, we just find two or three bits of bone, it doesn't matter what kind of bones they are or what the circumstances of the discoveries are, we fit them together and build a man or a woman from them, and then we create a complete life style for them. It's absolutely amazing what you can do with a few bones, a fertile imagination and a good artist. This is known as "reconstructions" Reconstruction are achieved by using this very active the imagination, drawing some pictures or building a model to look like the cross between man and monkey. We call these remarkable creatures "Missing links" Oh dear, another setback, the missing links are missing. That's OK; we will just make some up. I mean we might as well, since everything else is made up anyway. The media will help us get it over the line; they are excellent in creating a sensational story from nothing. All you need is a good headline.

CHAPTER 4

MISSING LINKS

**MISSING LINKS FOUND!
MAN'S APE ANCESTRY PROVEN!**

These kind of headlines have appeared in newspapers and magazines from time to time, Informing us that the discovery of various fossil bones are the missing links that proves that we descended from apes or monkeys, or, according to Darwin and one of his disciples Richard Dawkins, we probably even came from turnips. However, when we look closely at some of these discoveries, we find some amazing facts.

Here are just a few examples.

The Piltdown man:

Was found in a gravel pit in Sussex England in 1912, it was considered to be the second most important fossil proving the evolution of man—It was exposed as a complete forgery 41 years later. The skull was of modern age, the fragments had been chemically stained to give the appearance of age and the teeth had been filed down.

Java man:

in 1891 Eugene Dubois the Dutch paleoanthropologist / geologist, discovered remains of what he described as "a species in between humans and apes." However the find, consisted of only a skullcap, a few teeth, and a femur. The femur was found 50 feet away from the original skullcap a full year later.

Let's look at a living so called "missing link"

Ota Benga: "The pygmy in the zoo"

This man was a pygmy, no different from the pygmies we see today, he was married and had two children but he was exhibited in the Monkey House at the Bronx Zoo as part of a display intended to promote the concepts of human evolution.
The St. Louis Republic newspaper reported on the exhibit on March 6, 1904

It is a remarkable fact that both spontaneous generation and inherited acquired characteristics was destroyed by scientific research findings Here are some of them:

Francesco Redi 1668 the Italian Physician and poet was the first recorded person to seriously attack the idea of spontaneous generation. I was generally accepted at the time that maggots arose spontaneously in rotting meat.

Redi believed that maggots developed from eggs laid by flies. To test his hypothesis, he set out meat in a variety of flasks, some open to the air, some sealed completely, and others covered with gauze. As he had expected, maggots appeared only in the open flasks in which the flies could reach the meat and lay their eggs.

Louis Pasteur (1822–1895) disproved the theory of spontaneous generation in 1861, when he performed an experiment which proved that life cannot arise from non-living materials.

August Friedrich Leopold Weismann (1834–1914) a German biologist disproved Lamarck's "inheritance of acquired characteristics." theory. He cut off the tails of 901 young white mice over 19 consecutive generations, but each new generation continued to grow full-length tails.

People do not acquire inherited characteristics they need to be programmed into their gene pool from the very beginning. Characteristics are either there or they are not, you cannot add them or acquire them. Jewish males have been circumcised for thousands of years and yet every single male Jew is born with a foreskin.

Oh, dear! Spontaneous generation does not work; inheritance of acquired characteristics or natural selection does not work. As I said before, no matter how hard we try to put clothes on this poor bloke, we cannot seem to get anything to fit. Maybe, just maybe, this poor King is naked. Maybe, if we look even more closely with an open and innocent mind, we will discover the same thing as the little boy discovered in the story. The Emperor really has not got any clothes but this is getting really quite serious. It is becoming fairly obvious that we have not even got an Emperor to put clothes on, and we have been conned into believing a lie.

Chapter 5
The Real Reason

I hope by this time you will have recognized the complete nakedness of the theory of evolution. It would be good if that's all there was to it but it's not. The very sinister and dangerous reason for getting people to believe that this King and his clothes are real has nothing to do with whether the King or his clothes are real. It has nothing to do with convincing people that half-man half-ape creatures once lived in the past, or that fish turned into monkeys and monkeys turned into men. The real reason for the desperate attempt to convince us that evolution is scientific fact is:

TO REPLACE GOD!

If you have any doubt about the validity of this statement, have a look at this comment by;

Richard Lewontin. Evolutionary biologist and geneticist.

"We take the side of science in spite of the patent absurdity of some of its constructs, in spite of its failure to fulfill many of its extravagant promises, because we have a prior commitment, a commitment to materialism. Moreover, that materialism is an absolute for we cannot allow a Divine Foot in the door."

Destroy belief in God

The sole purpose of many evolutionists, for whatever reason, is to destroy belief in God. I am not saying that all evolutionists are even aware of this objective but, if you believe in evolution under any name, you don't believe in the God of the Bible who made the heavens and the earth and you and me. If you throw out the book of Genesis, you throw out the entire Bible. Evolutionary teaching and Christianity are total opposites. They are entirely incompatible. You cannot believe both teachings, or try to combine parts of the two. Anyone attempting to do so is simply fooling themselves.

Some of the most prominent evolutionists of our time such as Richard Lewontin and Richard Dawkins make it abundantly clear that their major objective is to destroy the teachings of the Bible which include the Jesus of Christianity and his claims to be the Son of God. Think about it, if you believe in evolution you are saying that the word God gave us in the scriptures is a lie. If you've got that wrong, you have a serious problem.

I wonder if Dawkins, Lewontin, and their like-minded cronies, ever take the time to think about what would happen if they were successful. What would happen if we all decided that the Bible was a lie? Have you thought about it? Have you ever really wondered where we would be if belief in God totally disappeared?

The first thing that would happen would be to leave a spiritual and moral vacuum for all sorts of substitutes to take its place. It would create a vacuum that would be filled with the religions of Communism, Fascism, National Socialism, or some other "ism" whose laws are made and changed at the whim of the current dictator. We would soon find out that the suggestion by Richard Dawkins in his book "The God Delusion" that all religions are the same, is a long way from the truth.

Let's have a look at what we can expect if the systems mentioned took the place of God. We have seen it all before, and the results were horrendous. There would be no need for morality and decent standards, just do as you like, or at least do as the current authority deems to be right. Let us get rid of Jews, Catholics could go as well, and we would not tolerate homosexuals, unless the current dictator was one. No one is safe under this sort of system. When children and youth are taught in school that they are a higher stage of animal, who needs moral principles? When we are all just animals, you can do whatever you want. Personal survival and success will come only by rivalry, killing off the weak so that only the strong survive.

Darwinism basically taught that our ancestors were animals and civilization only advanced by killing off the weak. During the Second World War, Nazism and Fascism declared that in the struggle to survive, the fittest will win out at the expense of their rivals. This led to extreme acts of racism.

I am just glancing at the news on TV while writing this section. Syria is getting blown to bits by a mad man who believes in the doctrine that the fittest and strongest will win, and they probably will. But where does that leave those people who do not agree with his or her dictatorial policies? . . . . DEAD. That is how it works. But what happens when somebody comes along who is stronger than the current dictator? More people get DEAD. And so it goes on. We cannot keep living like this, we need to have some ultimate authority to guide us, but as long as we keep believing in the survival of the fittest and have unscrupulous people willing to prove it, we will continually live in fear.

These are of some of the comments made by

Joseph Stalin, Communist leader of Russia.

Death is the solution to all problems. No man—no problem. Staling executed millions who disagreed with his policies.

Everyone imposes his own system as far as his army can reach.

The death of one man is a tragedy. The death of millions is a statistic.

Benito Mussolini, Fascist dictator of Italy.

was also captivated by Darwin and Nietzsche; who got his ideas from Darwin

Mussolini believed that violence is basic to social transformation
(*Encyclopedia Britannica, 1962, Vol. 16, p.27).

Some of Mussolini's quotes:

Democracy is beautiful in theory; in practice it is a fallacy.

Fascism is a religion. The twentieth century will be known in history as the century of Fascism.

Let us have a dagger between our teeth, a bomb in our hands, and an infinite scorn in our hearts.

National Socialism; or Nazism, (historically also Hitlerism), was the ideology and practice of the Nazi Party of Nazi Germany It was a unique variety of Fascism that incorporated biological racism and anti-Semitism.

Adolf Hitler was chancellor and later dictator of Nazi Germany from 1933 to 1945. He carefully studied the writings of *Darwin and *Nietzsche. Hitler's book,

Mein Kampf, (My struggle) was based on evolutionary theory
*(*Sir ArthurKeith, Evolution and Ethics, 1947, p. 28).*

Hitler was determined to produce Germany's "Master Race by eliminating unfavorable individuals and inferior races such as Jews and Gypsies and anyone else who did not agree with him. The trouble with this sort of thinking is that everybody believes that their race is the only one that can be allowed to survive.

Some of the atrocities Hitler committed in Poland were horrendous. Polish citizens where literally dumped in one spot without work or accommodation, property and businesses were stolen to accommodate the arrival of imported Germans. Hitler is not the only person in modern history who has resorted to these methods. Others include Stalin, Idi Amin, Pol Pot and many more. Surely this should be a lesson to us to never permit this sort of dictatorship to get a foothold ever again. That is what can happen when you take God (the ultimate authority) out of the picture.

Key elements of the Nazi ideology

Racism: Especially anti-Semitism, which resulted in the Holocaust.

Anti-Slavism: Belief in the dominance of the White, Germanic, Aryan or Nordic races.

Eugenics which discouraged reproduction by anyone presumed to have inheritable undesirable traits

The denunciation of democracy, elimination of political parties, labour unions, and free press.

Social Darwinism.

Social forces that produce evolutionary progress through the natural conflicts between social groups. (the 'survival of the fittest').

Chapter 6

The Consequences

Can you imagine the chaos with all these systems fighting to fill the vacuum left by the demise of God?

What would be the point of morality or "Thou shalt not steal" and "Thou shalt not kill". Think about the one that says "Thou shalt not commit adultery". Some people say such an idea is old fashioned but look at the problems and heartache as a result of not following this one command, broken families, broken hearts, even leading to the downfall of governments. It can be the cause of physical violence, sexually transmitted diseases such as AIDS, syphilis, gonorrhea etc. It's all negative. I see on the news a member of parliament is on the verge of prosecution the result of which could bring down a Government due to breaking one of these old fashioned commandments. Thou shalt not commit adultery. Or at least thou shalt not use taxpayers' money to pay for it.

All the safety measures that have been instituted by the 10 commandments (provided for our protection) would be gone, no need for them, we will work out our own salvation. This is what's commonly known as anarchy.

When you make an unthinking comment or hold the popular belief that we all came from monkeys, have you any idea what you are letting yourself in for? Have you any idea the depth of that belief and what the consequences really are? It's all very well to say, "I don't believe all that rubbish about the Bible and God and creation. It's all a fairy tale". If that's what you believe, then you have every right in the world to believe and say that. But, if that _is_ your decision, you need to be aware that with every decision you have ever made or ever will make, whether you like it or not, there are consequences. When the consequences are as serious as eternal life or eternal death, you had better be sure you get it right.

No matter what your decision is, you can't change the facts. I remember when my kids were very young, I used to ask them silly questions, just for fun. One of those questions was:

"If you called a dog's tale a leg, how many legs would the dog have? Some of them, without really thinking about it, said 5. But the fact is, it doesn't matter what you call the dog's tail, it's always a tail. You can call it Donald Duck if you like, but it doesn't change the fact that it is a dog's tail. And, if the fact is, that the account of creation, as written in "Genesis", the first book of the Bible, is correct, then all the claims by the evolutionists, no matter how loud and how often they are made, will never change this fact and you lose big time.

From those who know how it works:

Adolf Hitler said "Make the lie big, make it simple, keep saying it, and eventually they will believe it"

Joseph Goebbels Reich Minister of Propaganda in Nazi Germany "If you tell a lie big enough and keep repeating it, people will eventually come to believe it. The lie can be maintained only for such time as the State can shield the people from the political, economic and/or military consequences of the lie. It thus becomes vitally important for the State to use all of its powers to repress dissent, for the truth is the mortal enemy of the lie, and thus by extension, the truth is the greatest enemy of the State."

Think exist.com

By believing in Evolution what do you have to gain? You came from nothing; you will go back to nothing, you might have a wonderful life just now, but when you die, is that all there is? Is it all over? Maybe that suits you fine and of course if it that's your choice then you have every right in the world to make that choice. If you choose to believe the evolution story and not believe in the promises in the Bible. (You can't have it both ways, this is not a two bob each way bet) then you are disregarding the possibility that you could spend eternity in a place so beautiful and safe that you cannot even imagine. This is how Paul puts it in his letter to the Corinthians

1 Corinthians 2:9
NKJV

But as it is written: "Eye has not seen, nor ear heard, Nor has it entered into the heart of man The things which God has prepared for those who love Him."

And from the Old testament book of Isaiah 64:4
21st Century King James Version (KJ21)

For since the beginning of the world men have not heard nor perceived by the ear, neither hath the eye seen, O God, besides thee, what He hath prepared for him that wait for Him.

This is what the Bible promises, so when I consider the following statement it really amazes me.

The Bible is a collection of 66 books written by different authors at different times and in different geographical locations all conveying the same message. Its major theme is the coming of a messiah at a specific time in history who promises us everlasting life. This was fulfilled with the coming of Jesus, His crucifixion and His resurrection, all of which were forecast centuries before He was even born and who makes eternal life a real possibility. This is what the Bible is all about and, incidentally, has changed the lives of millions of people, from all walks and stations in life, throughout the world and throughout the centuries.

When you consider how humans are generally such an inquisitive mob, you would think that we would at least want to consider a book that claims how a much greater existence could be attained after this one. The Bible teaches that eternal life is a real possibility. I cannot understand why so many people, refuse to take the 66 books of the Bible as seriously as they would take any other book of historical fact. After all, no-one is going to lose anything by doing so and they may stand to gain a great deal.

Why in the world would anyone in their right mind pass up the chance of living forever in paradise?

People take all kinds of risks and play against enormous odds in the hope that they might win the lottery or beat the pokies to possibly get a better quality of life for a few years or even weeks. Yet they discard the chance of obtaining life in paradise forever without any risk. That is what the Bible offers. I find it almost unbelievable that people can pass up such a fantastic offer without giving it a lot of thought. Now here's the thing, you are an individual, you will make that choice. Ask yourself what have I got to lose?

Again my attention is drawn to an event that is happening this week, 8/05/2012, in Australia. I was passing a Newsagent in our local Shopping Centre today. There was a massive queue for almost 50 meters outside the shop. When I asked my wife if she knew what was going on. She told me it was for a ticket in the 7 million dollar lotto or lottery. There are probably millions of those queues all over the country, people willing to risk their hard earned money on probably a 70 million to one chance of winning.

Why not give yourself a fighting chance and bet on something that costs you nothing and if you win it's worth more than all the money that could ever be made?

Whether you like it or not, you are, at this very moment, making some sort of decision. There's no middle ground on this one. You are either in it or you are out of it. You are deciding whether you will either throw this in the rubbish bin or read on and find out if there is anything that might help you to take your decision to another level.

Let's have a look at some of the scientific evidence that formed my reason for taking my position. This is by no means exhaustive.

CHAPTER 7

THE LIVING CELL

The living cell. Read the following passage and with an open, intelligent, and extremely sophisticated machine like your brain, ask yourself: did this come about by sheer accident? And if it didn't, then how in the world did it happen?

In 1839 Matthias Jakob Schleiden and Theodor Schwann, discovered some amazing facts about what was previously regarded as a simple living cell. They found that the cell was not simple at all but was a highly complicated piece of machinery. Schleiden and Schwann also identified that all organisms are composed of one or more cells that come from preexisting cells. Vital functions of an organism occur within cells, and that all cells contain the hereditary information necessary for regulating cell functions and for transmitting information to the next generation of cells. In other words the living cell is a machine.

Have a look at the following questions and think carefully and honestly before you answer them, Call on your own intelligence and experience to answer them. If you don't answer them truthfully, the only person you're fooling is yourself.

1. Have you ever seen anything coming from nothing?.
2. Have you ever seen even the simplest piece of machinery developing itself by accident?
3. Have you ever seen any evidence of one species changing to another species. I'm not talking about small dogs changing into bigger dogs: they are still dogs. Likewise, smooth-haired cats changing into fluffy-haired cats: they are still cats. I'm talking about any evidence of a monkey, whatever variety of monkey, changing into a man, or even into another type of monkey or even a dogs tail changing into leg just because we called it a leg.

There is no evidence whatsoever of any of these things ever happening although scientists have spent much time and money to find such evidence. That's why they need to invent fakes such as the Piltdown man Java Man and many others. This is where I have heard some people getting really angry and defensive and claim with great passion that there is abundant evidence of this happening. Where is it?

Let's have a look at question 2.

2. When have you ever seen even the simplest piece of machinery developing itself by accident? The answer is quite certain that you haven't.

Wooden boxes for example, think about the steps it takes to make a wooden box

1. Wood, where did it come from? You have to find a tree, cut it down, shape it into the correct size panels to make the box the right size.
2. We need to find some nails, that in itself takes planning and effort to get the right size nails.
3. We need to find something to hammer the nails in with.
4. We need to measure and fit all the parts together.

That's only a simple wooden box and we are expected to believe that something as complicated as a living cell just happened. How do you think a complete complicated system like our immune system would come about?

Well let's see if, even using all the imagination you can muster, you can call this an accident.

The Blood Cells: Through an electron microscope we can get a close up look at these remarkable little cells that make up the human blood.

The white blood cells at first glance look like a shapeless piece of jelly, it's a bit spooky, it slithers along your veins something like a very slow moving snail but when bacteria gets into the body "Shazam" in a flash these lazy little cells turn into Captain Marvel, Superman and Batman. They go into action attacking the invader as part of a deadly army. When these little blokes get to the scene of the battle, they have some pretty deadly artillery:

The "neutrophils: These are the foot soldiers. There are millions of them, they literally smother the enemy and disintegrate it and then die having reproduced millions more to continue the fight when needed.

The macrophages: The storm troopers. As soon as the battle commences they suddenly blow up to as much as ten times their size. They ambush the enemy and eat about one hundred of them in less than a second. They also fuse together to form a giant cell then shoot the enemy down with enzymes.

The lymphocytes: The different types are designed to assassinate the different types of bacteria. The B cell lymphocyte is absolutely fatal they send out guided missiles called antibodies.

You cannot possibly believe that this highly organized army came about by accident one step at a time. I mean, it's easy to say we gradually evolved from apes one step at a time, but that is a very glib viewpoint. You need to look at the whole picture. It had to be planned by an intelligent mind. You simply cannot get that kind of complicated system happening by a whole series of accidents.

What was the question? When have you ever seen even the simplest piece of machinery or a complex system like the army of blood cells developing by accident? This is not rocket science it's just plain and simple common sense. The problem with common sense is that people complicate it.

If you think the living cell is complicated, have a look at D.N.A.

Inside each cell in your body is a nucleus which contains complex mechanisms such as chromosomes. These chromosomes contain genes. Inside the genes is the complicated chemical structure we call DNA. Each gene has a thousand or more such DNA units within it. Each cell contains tens of thousands of such genes grouped into 23 pairs of chromosomes. Inside the DNA is the total of all the genetic possibilities for a given species. This is called the gene pool of genetic traits or genome, which stores all the traits your species can have.

In contrast, the specific sub-code for YOU is the genotype which is the code for all the possible inherited features you could have. The genotype is the individual's code. **WOW!!!** And this is only a fraction of the whole system.

If you think all that happens by accident, you have a lot more faith than I have.

The discovery of the DNA molecule in 1953 has had an enormous effect on biological research. It has also caused a major predicament for evolutionary scientists. It provides clear evidence that every species is locked into its own coding pattern making it impossible for one species to change into another. It shows quite clearly that a species can vary within its own group i.e. big dogs small dogs etc. but one species cannot jump from one to another. The mathematical possibility of producing the correct DNA code for any one species accidentally is nonexistent. If you can imagine getting 12 one dollar coins and throwing them in the air and they all came down balanced on their edge. You have the same chance of a correct DNA molecule for any species being produced accidentally.

The full implications of DNA, seriously challenges the theory of evolution. Evolutionists refuse to accept that this incredibly complex structure was actually designed by an intelligent mind, instead, they have come up with the totally astonishing claim, that all the complicated DNA in every life-form made itself out of dirty water and a lightning storm.

It is similar to the "coming from nothing" theory with just a little bit of extra cloth and a bit more colour. Apparently the lightning hit the dirty water and made living creatures complete with DNA, with their entire genetic code built in. They were able to move about, to eat, digest food and get rid of the waste out of their system. (By the way, there is no such thing as simple life: all forms of life are more complicated than human intelligence can understand). That same stroke of lightning made both male and female and provided them with the ability get together to produce offspring and they in turn, more offspring etc. This is the evolutionary formula for making life, concluding in the following fascinating theory: Dirt + water + time = living creatures.

Can you honestly believe that the above formula can enable everything about us to make itself, when we know that man-made things such as houses, cars, even wooden boxes require planning, intelligent design and careful workmanship. Surely everything in nature such as the bumble bee, the human eye, the heart and ear cannot be the result of accidents, random confusion, and time.

The DNA code and the components of protein are so utterly complicated that they defy any possibility that they could have been produced by chance events. Yet, evolutionists tell us that random actions are the only kind of occurrences which have ever been used to accomplish the work of evolution. For life to form in the first place it would require that highly exacting code to be in place on the very first day. Thereafter each new species would require to have all its highly exacting code to be in place as well right from the start. Nothing can evolve from one species to another. There is no evidence of it ever happening.

Why are they so desperate for us to believe that we evolved from nothing? It doesn't make any sense. Unless the objective is simply. Dare I say it again?

TO REPLACE GOD

Let's face it, this is what evolution is all about, it does not matter whether your belief is in theistic evolution which is simply a tool that God employed to develop human life and then left it to evolve by natural means or you believe that we just accidentally happened as a result of something still to be determined. Neither of these theories is in harmony with the Biblical account.

In 1953 Stanley Miller produced a few amino acids from chemicals, using a small sparking apparatus to replicate lightning. This created a flurry in the newspaper who declared: "Life has been created!" But that wasn't quite the whole truth. What did happen was that instead of proving that life could be created accidentally, they actually did the opposite and disproved the possibility that evolution could occur. The experiment proved that man-made production of amino acids would result in only left—and right-handed amino acids. However only left-handed amino acids exist in animals, neither man-made nor accidental production could ever produce a living creature. Incidentally the amino acids produced in Millers experiment were totally dead.

Honestly! When are we going to wake up to ourselves and recognize the truth?

So where are we with the king's clothes now? It would appear that both King evolution and his clothes are a complete figment of someone's overly active imagination. If we are to make a decision about whether we believe that this planet and all that is in it including you and me came about by chance, or that the whole, complicated, sophisticated, balanced structure was created by an intelligent mind, what's it going to be?

EARLY WARNINGS—Over a century and a half ago Johann von Goethe, made a profound statement.

"Science has been seriously retarded by the study of what is not worth knowing."—
Johann von Goethe (1749-1832), quoted in Asimov's Book of Science and Nature Quotations, p. 257.

It would have been well if Charles Darwin and his disciples had paid attention to this warning. Thousands of people possibly millions throughout the world have been seriously damaged by Darwin and his followers.

After the book, "Origin of Species" was published, many highly regarded men warned Darwin of the dangers that would result if the evolution theory were to become widely accepted.

George Romanes a personal friend of Darwin wrote to him expressing his grave concern about the consequences of the publication:

"Never in the history of man has so terrific a calamity befallen the race as that which all who look may now behold advancing as a deluge, black with destruction, resistless in might, uprooting our most cherished hopes, engulfing our most precious creed, and burying our highest life in mindless desolation. The flood-gates of infidelity are open, and Atheism overwhelming is upon us."
George Romanes, A Candid Examination of Theism (1878).

Soon after "The Origin of Species", was published, Adam Sedgwick, author of the famous "Student's Text Book of Zoology", wrote to Darwin. Noting the ridiculous non-scientific "facts" and hypotheses in the

"The Origin of Species", Sedgwick expressed his opinion to Darwin in the following words: "I have read your book with more pain than pleasure. Parts of it I admired greatly, parts I laughed till my sides were almost sore, other parts I read with absolute sorrow because I think them utterly false and grievously mischievous".

CHAPTER 8

HYPOTHESIS, THEORY
OR
SCIENTIFIC FACT

I am totally convinced that, in harmony with the evidence available, evolution is absolutely nothing more than an Hypothesis leading to a philosophy. This Hypothesis has taken on the status of some sort of "Sacred Cow" it has become immune to criticism; it is even absolved from enquiry. The growing opposition to it is not only ignored, it is attacked either viciously or with ridicule. Some of Richard Dawkins comments for example are beyond ridiculous. "Fairies at the bottom of the garden", The great Spaghetti god in the Skye" These comments are designed to get the support of an audience, not to seriously debate the real issue, which simply asks: Is macro evolution scientific fact?

Let's have a look at how one reliable source describes science and what is required to establish scientific fact.

The Oxford American Dictionary (1982) definition of science describes

Science, as a branch of study which is considered either a connected body of demonstrated truths or observed facts systematically classified and more or less colligated and brought under general laws which includes trustworthy methods for the discovery of new truth within its own domain.

The scientific method is applied by:

1) Observing and recording certain natural phenomena
2) A generalization (scientific hypothesis) is formulated, based on observations
3) This generalization allows predictions to be made
4) The hypothesis is then tested by conducting experiments to determine if the predicted results are consistent
5) If the predictions prove true, then the hypothesis is considered verified.
6) Through continual confirmation of the predictions (individually or by other parties) the hypothesis will become a theory.
7) The theory with time and tests will graduate to scientific law.

What this generally accepted definition of science and the scientific method indicates is that evolution does not comply with the true scientific method, it is simply

a) Unknown organisms
b) Arising from unknown chemicals

c) Produced in an atmosphere or ocean of unknown composition
d) Under unknown conditions
e) Which organisms have climbed an unknown evolutionary ladder.
f) By an unknown process
g) Offering unproven evidence

In other words, scientific fact requires the presence of demonstrated truths or observed facts, the absence of which concludes that the evolutionary theory is not scientific fact, but rather a philosophy.

So why in the world are we teaching evolution in schools as scientific fact?

This is not education. Educators and parents alike have a massive responsibility to ensure that future generations are being taught facts. We cannot do this properly unless we are aware of the facts ourselves. The one fact that cannot be stated too often is that evolution is not scientific fact, no matter how loud you shout it, no matter how often you say it, the fact remains that, evolution is not scientific fact.

Many diligent scientists who have spent years trying to work with the evolution theory, have concluded that it simply does not work and they want it rejected entirely. We need to consider the overwhelming mass of evidence in opposition to it. We need to stop being terrified by the strategies used by evolutionary evangelicals. We need to say STOP show me the evidence.

Evolutionists explain their objective

Here are some of the reasons why evolutionists want to stick to a theory that has no evidence to support it, one which has been repeatedly disproved. This is why some people cling so fanatically to a lie.

Objective: Separation from God

Evolutionary thought is popular because it is a world view which allows us to get God out of the picture and claim complete autonomy for our actions.

Objective: Sexual freedom.

This behavior has become the norm for people who want to make their own rules, If nobody finds out about it and you can get off with it, just do it. The problem is, we need to be aware that there are literary thousands of examples of how dangerous this practice has proved to be. But that's the way they want it, so let's adopt the evolution theory. That'll fix it . . . . AS IF!!!

Objective: A way to hide from God.

Right in the very beginning, when man had sinned for the first time he did something:

Genesis 3: 8

<u>And</u> they heard the sound of the Lord God walking in the garden in the cool of the day, and Adam and his

wife <u>hid themselves</u> from the presence of the Lord God among the trees of the garden.

So what's new, we are still doing the same thing today.

THE BEST EVIDENCES FOR EVOLUTION

Evolutionists have come up with some fascinating reasons why they believe evolution to be true. Here are five of these inspired utterances:

1—**We know that evolution is true because living things have parents.**

"No one has ever found an organism that is known not to have parents, or a parent. This is the strongest evidence on behalf of evolution."—

Tom Bathell, "Agnostic Evolutionists, "Harper's, February 1985, p. 81.

2—**We know that evolution is true because living things have children.**

C.H. Waddington, quoted by Tom Bethell, in "The Mistake," Harper's Magazine, February 1978, p. 75.

3—**We know that evolution is true because there are perfections**.

David M. Raup, "Conflicts between Darwin and Paleontology," Bulletin of the Field Museum of Natural History, January 1979, pp. 25-28. 859 The Evolution Cruncher

4—**We know that evolution is true because there are imperfections.**

"If there were no imperfections, there would be no evidence to favor evolution by natural selection over creation."

Jeremy Cherfas, "The Difficulties of Darwinism," New Scientist, Vol. 102 (May 17, 1984), p. 29.

5—We know that evolution is true because species become extinct.

David Raup, "Conflicts between Darwin and Paleontology," Field Museum of Natural History Bulletin, January 1979, p. 29.

Does that seem to be just a little bit confusing? There is absolutely no consistency in this, in fact I can't find any consistency anywhere in the whole evolutionary story. It keeps changing depending on who is telling the story.

But have a look at this little story that was written about 6000 years ago, it has never changed, it is perfectly straight forward, there is no ambiguity about it and again it comes from the first book of the Bible

Genesis1:1. In the beginning God created the heavens and the earth.

This is the very first chapter of the very first book of God's word, The Bible.

I ask you, please look at this statement, read it over a couple of times and then read the following statement by the current hero of evolution, the supreme leader of the evolutionary cause._Professor Richard Dawkins in his book entitled "The greatest show on earth" Dawkins remarks:

> Evolution is a fact. Beyond reasonable doubt, beyond serious doubt, beyond sane, informed, intelligent doubt, beyond doubt evolution is a fact. The evidence for evolution is at least as strong as the evidence for the Holocaust, even allowing for eye witnesses to the Holocaust. It is the plain truth that we are cousins of chimpanzees, somewhat more distant cousins of monkeys, more distant cousins still of aardvarks and manatees, yet more distant cousins of bananas and turnips . . . continue the list as long as desired. That didn't have to be true. It is not self-evidently, tautologically, obviously true, and there was a time when most people, even educated people, thought it wasn't. It didn't have to be true, but it is. We know this because a rising flood of evidence supports it. Evolution is a fact, and this book will demonstrate it. No reputable scientist disputes it, and no unbiased reader will close the book doubting it.

I feel positively embarrassed reading this, it's hard to imagine that this rambling nonsense came from an Oxford University Professor. Now go back and read the first chapter of Genesis. Does the word sanity come to mind?

In his book "The Greatest Show on Earth" when explaining the Origins of Life. Dawkins writes in chapter 13,

<u>We have no evidence</u> about what the first step in making life was, but we do know the kind of step <u>it must have been</u>. <u>It must have been whatever it took to get natural selection started</u>. Before that first step, the sorts of improvement that only natural selection can achieve were impossible. And that means the key step was the rising, <u>by some process as yet unknown</u>, of a self-replicating entity.

This sort of pomposity is typical of Dawkins logic; it is not even close to evidence of evolution. If evolution is to be taught, it should be taught as a theory, not as scientific fact—at least until it has some scientific fact to back it up. Look at the statements I have underlined

<u>"We have no evidence"</u>
<u>"It must have been"</u>.
<u>"It must have been whatever it took to get natural selection started"</u>
<u>"some process as yet unknown"</u>,

What in the world kind of scientific fact is that? I sometimes wonder if Richard Dawkins is really serious. I mean, how could, a supposedly intelligent Oxford Scholar write this kind of stuff. It's the kind of argument you would expect from a 10 year old kid and not a very bright one at that. I often wonder, whose side is this guy on? If I had an advocate like this arguing my case in court, I would either plead guilty or insanity. It fascinates me that he has the audacity to call people who believe in creation "stupid".

CHAPTER 9

EVOLUTION QUESTIONED

For over 120 years, evolutionary scientists have been trying to work out how evolution occurred, but it's a bit like the Kings clothes, they cannot get anything to fit. Spontaneous generation never happened, Natural selection has never been witnessed. Lamarckism is just a piece of nonsense. Nobody can decide whether it happened over millions of years (Phyletic gradualism) or if it happened in short bursts (Punctuated equilibrium).

Ambrose Fleming, president, British Association for Advancement of Science, put it very simply in his book "The Unleashing of Evolutionary Thought" When he said, "Evolution is baseless and quite incredible".

Pierre-Paul Grasse, a leading French scientist throws his hat in the ring stating that "the Evolutionary theory is nothing more than a myth and concerned scientists recognize that it needs to be obliterated in order for science to progress".

The evolution myth has been a real frustration for me. I cannot understand why otherwise intelligent people accept these teachings when there is so little evidence to back them up. I do not understand why people do not recognize the weaknesses in the evolution arguments which have been put forward as established truths.

I also get frustrated and confused when I learn about some scientists who admit that there is no evidence for the evolution theory, but they are unwilling to consider any other possibility Charles Singer Director of a large graduate biology department is one of them. Dr. George Wald is another. This leads me to the conclusion that the only reason they and thousands of others accept the theory is because they want to. It has nothing to do with evidence. No matter how much evidence they find, they will never accept or admit that we were created by God

Charles Singer has this to say:

"Evolution is perhaps unique among major scientific theories in that the appeal for its acceptance is not that there is evidence of it, but that any other proposed interpretation of the data is wholly incredible."
Charles Singer, A Short History of Science to the Nineteenth Century, 1941.

He openly admits that there is no evidence for it. What more do you need? There are many evolutionary scientists who have a very uncomfortable feeling about the validity of the theory due to the fact that there is no reliable evidence. There are also many people who just do not think about it enough, but simply go with the flow and accept whatever is dished up to them. If you are one of these people I urge you to think for yourself, ask the question, where's the evidence, and if there is none, why do they keep on passionately pushing this empty barrow?

There are many scientists who defend this unsupported theory. This is using up valuable resources time and talent that could be better employed in other more productive areas.

I recently watched a documentary movie called the "Nazi Titanic". Joseph Goebbels Reich Minister of Propaganda in Nazi Germany was making a movie about the sinking of the Titanic from a Nazi perspective. This was an effort to compete with Hollywood in film making. One of the weaknesses he encountered was that much of the super talent, Directors and Producers that could have been used, had either been sent to concentration camps because they were Jews, or had escaped to other countries including America where they were eagerly sought by Hollywood. I suggest that the same sort of waste is happening today with talented scientists wasting their time trying to prove a theory that is unable to be proved.

Come on you scientists, you are wasting valuable time and talent defending this nonsense, Isn't it about time you recognized the hopelessness of this pursuit. You need to break the ties that bind you to this ridiculous theory. It is stifling the life out of you and holding you back. Let's face it, when you look at the evidence available, scientists who teach that evolution is a fact, are either very ill informed or con men. How in the world can you teach something when you do not have one scrap of evidence to back it up? Dr. T.N. Tahmisian. Atomic Energy Commission, called it a tangled mishmash of guessing games and figure juggling."

G.G. Simpson, a leading evolutionist writer of the mid-20th century tried harder than most evolutionists to defend evolution. But found it impossible to find the mechanism to make it work. Try as he did, he could not attribute evolution to any single cause.

CHAPTER 10

THE FOSSIL RECORD

Until now, we have dealt mainly with the theory of evolution in relation to Species changing from one species to another species. But let us have a look at the fundamental problem as we study the fossil record. Here we come upon a variety of very serious problems which undermine the strata/fossil theory. Fossils play a very important part in our study of evolution; they provide the only record of plants and animals in ancient times. The fossil record is extremely important and is often used to provide proof for evolution. All the evidence in these fossils should enable scientists to prove that one species has evolved from another. If this is not evident then the fossils are not a witness to evolution in the past. If such is the case, then there is no reason to believe that evolution has ever occurred.

The most important considerations are:

The Cambrian strata occur at the very bottom of all the strata (the geologic column). This is known as the "Cambrian explosion" and is filled with complex, multi-celled extinct life forms. These appear to have formed suddenly and simultaneously. There are no transitional species throughout the column. Nothing is changing to anything else. This produces the problem of fossil gaps or missing links. There is mixed up and out-of-order strata all over the place. Singly or together, they destroy the evolutionary argument from the rock strata. But that's not the only problem we find.

Complexity at the beginning, simplest just as complex:

Have you ever heard of trilobites? Trilobites are among the most common creatures found in the lowest part of the Cambrian strata; these little creatures belong to the same group as the insects (the arthropods). Yet they had extremely complex eyes. The lens structure of these little creatures is so complicated, that it took humans until the middle of the 20th century to replicate it for use in a camera. Remember, we are talking about one of the most common creatures at the very bottom of the fossil strata.

Science News 105, February 2, 1974, p. 72 declared that the trilobite had "the most sophisticated eye lenses ever produced by nature." So you have to ask yourself, if these little creatures are found in the lowest part of the Cambrian strata and their complicated eyes are fully developed, what did they evolve from? There really is only one answer to that question. The only sensible answer is, they didn't.

Here is how an expert describes it:

*Norman Macbeth, in a speech at Harvard University in 1983, said this:

"I have dealt with biologists over the last twenty years now. I have found that, in a way, they are hampered by having too much education. They have been steeped from their childhood in the Darwinian views, and, as a result, it has taken possession of their minds to such an extent that they are almost unable to see many facts that are not in harmony with Darwinism.

These facts simply aren't there for them and other ones are sort of suppressed or distorted. I'll give you some examples.

First, and perhaps most important, is the first appearance of fossils. This occurs at a time called the 'Cambrian,' these fossils appear at that time in the Cambrian in a pretty highly developed form. They don't start very low and evolve bit by bit over long periods of time. In the lowest fossil-bearing strata of all [the Cambrian, they are already there, and are pretty complicated in more-or-less modern form.

One example of this is the little animal called the trilobite. There are a great many fossils of the trilobite right there at the beginning with no buildup to it, no evolution of life-forms leading to it and, if you examine them closely, you will find that they are not simple animals, they are small, but they have an eye that has been discussed a great deal in recent years, an eye that is simply incredible, It is made up of dozens of little tubes which are all at slightly different angles so that it covers the entire field of vision with a different tube pointing at each spot on the horizon. But these tubes are a lot more complicated than that, they have a lens on them that is optically arranged in a very complicated way and it is bound into another layer that has to be just exactly right for them to see anything.

The more complicated it is, the less likely it is simply to have grown up out of nothing. This situation has troubled everybody from the beginning to have everything at the very opening of the drama. The curtain goes up life-forms first appear in the Cambrian strata and you have the players on the stage already, entirely in modern costumes."

*Norman Macbeth, Speech at Harvard University, September 24,1983, quoted in L.D. Sunderland, Darwin's Enigma (1988), p. 150.

Riccardo Levi-Setti, one of the world's leading trilobite researchers wrote:

"Each eye of the trilobite had two lenses In fact, this optical doublet is a device so typically associated with human invention that its discovery in trilobites comes as something of a shock. The realization that trilobites developed and used such devices half a billion years ago, makes the shock even greater. And a final discovery that the refracting interface between the two lens elements in a trilobite's eye was designed ["designed"] in accordance with optical constructions worked out by Descartes and Huygens in the mid-seventeenth century—borders on sheer science fiction.

The design of the trilobite's eye lens could well qualify for a patent disclosure."—
*(*Riccardo Levi-Setti, Trilobites, 2nd ed., University of Chicago Press, 1993, pp. 54, 57.*

We find extremely complicated creatures at the very beginning of the story, with absolutely nothing leading up to them, nothing to indicate that any creature has ever changed from one to another. You would think that, in light of this sort of compelling evidence that the anti-God fraternity would come up with a better way to turn people away from God than trying to sell the evolution story. Once again it absolutely amazes me that someone can invent a story like this and you get so many people willing to believe it. What they have attempted to do is to attack Gods word right at the beginning. Think about it, if you want to bring down a very large building, where would you attack it? Right at the very foundations and that is exactly what they have done.

If you are determined to believe this evolution story, the only reason you believe it, is because you want to. It certainly has nothing to do with science or fact and if you think for one minute that Darwin or Dawkins or any of the other evolutionary disciples are the force behind it you are way off the mark. Let us consider the real force behind it, the real power that gives these people the energy and the drive to continually promote the myth. The identity of this force or power comes straight from the Bible, a set of documents, 66 books in all, that have been around for between 2 and 6 thousand years, have never changed in all that time, have been attacked, burned and banned by all sorts of authorities throughout the ages and is still referred to today more than any other set of documents ever written. This is what it says:

Ephesians 6:12. NKJV For we do not wrestle against flesh and blood, but against principalities, against powers, against the rulers of the darkness of this age, against spiritual hosts of wickedness in the heavenly places.

This is the force we are dealing with and I would advise you very strongly, do not take this lightly.

Isaiah 53
21st Century King James Version (KJ21)

1. Who hath believed our report? And to whom is the arm of the Lord revealed?
2. For He shall grow up before Him as a tender plant, and as a root out of a dry ground. He hath no form nor comeliness, and when we shall see Him, there is no beauty that we should desire Him.
3. He is despised and rejected of men, a Man of sorrows, and acquainted with grief. And we hid as it were our faces from Him; He was despised, and we esteemed Him not.
4. Surely He hath borne our grief and carried our sorrows; yet we did esteem Him stricken, smitten of God, and afflicted.
5. But He was wounded for our transgressions; He was bruised for our iniquities. The chastisement of our peace was upon Him, and with His stripes we are healed.

6. All we like sheep have gone astray; we have turned everyone to his own way; and the Lord hath laid on Him the iniquity of us all.

7. He was oppressed, and He was afflicted, yet He opened not his mouth; He is brought as a lamb to the slaughter; and as a sheep before her shearers is dumb, so He opened not His mouth.

8. He was taken from prison and from judgment; and who shall declare His generation? For He was cut off out of the land of the living; for the transgression of my people was He stricken.

9. He made His grave with the wicked, and with the rich in His death, because He had done no violence, neither was any deceit in His mouth.

10. Yet it pleased the Lord to bruise Him; He hath put Him to grief. When thou shalt make His soul an offering for sin, He shall see His seed, He shall prolong His days, and the pleasure of the Lord shall prosper in His hand.

11. He shall see of the travail of His soul, and shall be satisfied. By His knowledge shall My righteous Servant justify many, for He shall bear their iniquities.

12. Therefore will I divide Him a portion with the great, and He shall divide the spoil with the strong, because He hath poured out His soul unto death. He was numbered with the transgressors; and He bore the sin of many, and made intercession for the transgressors.

You may not be aware of this, but this is exactly what happened to Jesus at His crucifixion, and it was written 600 years before He was born. There was another message written in these documents, 2000 years ago. A message that is as prevalent today as it was the day it was written. Read it and learn.

1 Corinthians 1:18. The message of the cross is foolishness to those who are perishing, but to us who are being saved it is the power of God.

This is powerful stuff. This has the authority that you will never find in the wishy washy mishmash that you read in the evolution story.

We need to get this whole thing in some sort of order and ask some really pertinent questions:

Did life come about as a result of spontaneous generation?
No it did not.

Do species change from one to another?
All the available evidence says no, they do not.

Is there evidence in the fossil record that species went through a process of evolution?
No there is no evidence of this ever happening.

That leaves us with one more area to examine.

How did the universe get started in the first place?

The most popular theory of course is the:

Chapter 11

Big Bang Theory

This is an attempt to describe what happened at the very beginning of our universe. The origin of the Big Bang theory can be credited to Edwin Hubble who observed that the universe is continually expanding in every direction.

These discoveries have shown beyond a reasonable doubt that our universe did have a beginning, prior to that moment there was nothing, during and after that moment there was something:

The big bang theory is an effort to explain what happened during and after that moment. The accepted theory suggests that our universe sprang into existence as a "singularity" around 13.7 billion years ago.

What is a "singularity" . . . . Well, to be honest, we don't know for sure

Where does it come from? We don't know that either

Why did it appear? . . . . It's a good question but we have no idea.

Singularities are thought to be areas of intense gravitational pressure which exist at the core of "black holes, but they defy our current comprehension of physics.

The theory suggests that the Universe began as an infinitesimally small, infinitely hot, infinitely dense, something (a singularity) but we have no idea where it came from. Many tend to imagine the singularity as a little fireball appearing somewhere in space, but according to the many experts, space didn't exist prior to the Big Bang.

Many scientists suggest that the Big Bang theory started with a giant explosion. Others however reject this idea and postulate that there was (and continues to be) an expansion similar to an extremely small balloon expanding to the size of our current universe.

The theory makes no attempt to explain how structures like stars and galaxies formed in the universe. The one thing that we can be sure of is that at one time none of these things existed and neither did we and now we are inside of it. Since it is impossible to be absolutely certain of how all of this came about, I think it is a fair question to ask: could it possibly have been created by an intelligent mind?

If that is possible, then what was it? Does God Exist?

OH! There is one other very important question that we have not mentioned. We need to find another essential component that gets us going and keeps going.

THE BREATH OF LIFE.

Think about it, <u>think about it very seriously.</u> Without the breath of life, we have nothing. We don't exist. Where are we going to find it?

Well there you have it. I have investigated every road I can find to try to verify the claim that evolution is scientific fact and I honestly have found no such evidence. What's the point of continually claiming that "there is abundant evidence that evolution is scientific fact" when there is nothing to back it up? It's all too negative, we came from nothing we are going nowhere. What's the point? Why bother getting up in the morning?

Can we leave all this negative stuff behind us for a while and look at some really positive aspects of life?

THE POSITIVELY REAL FACTS

I would like to share with you something that you can really hang your hat on, something that is a lot more positive than the evolutionary stuff we have looked at before and something that can only be explained by the presence of God. It's about a couple of really weird things that happened to me.

In 1988 I was quite a different person than I am today, I was a very heavy drinker, in fact I was an alcoholic and I was smoking about 20-30 cigarettes a day. It was ruining my life. I tried many times to give it up and every time I tried, I would to wake up in the middle of the night sweating like a pig. That was when I met a lady who introduced me to the Seventh-day Adventist church. I was talking to her at work one day after having a pretty heavy night on the booze the night before. After we had a bit of a discussion about my previous nights activities, she said to me "Do you know John, that your body is a temple of the Holy Spirit" and then she said something else but I didn't hear what it was and then she turned and walked away.

I didn't think much about it at the time but a couple of weeks later, I stopped smoking and drinking and started to attend the Seventh-day Adventist Church in Kingston a suburb south of Brisbane. That lasted for about 3 weeks and then I was back to the booze and smokes again and this time I really hit it with a vengeance every couple of days I was writing myself off. Then something really strange happened, I went into a shop in Beenleigh, another suburb south of Brisbane. I bought a packet of cigarettes and then this man came and spoke to me the conversation went like this:

"How ya goin"? He asked

"good mate". I replied

"Haven't seen you for a while" he remarked

I said "do I know you"?"

"Probably not" he said, "you went to church at Kingston"

I said "yeah I did but it's not my style"

"You've got a bit of a problem haven't you?"

I don't know whether I was confused or stunned. I wasn't really sure what was going on but I started to talk to this guy.

"Yes" I said "I've got a bit of a problem with the Grog".

Now this conversation went on for about 20 minutes but I can't remember exactly all the details. In the end he said "I have a message for you, the Lord wants you to talk to Him. Go to your bedroom and kneel down and tell the Lord that you cannot do this on your own; you need Him to do it for you. Will you do that"? I said yes, yes I will and he walked away. That was on a Friday afternoon.

The following Sunday night I was sitting watching TV and drinking a bottle of beer, suddenly I got this thought in my head, no voices, no bright lights, just a thought. I got up and went to my room and knelt down and prayed exactly the prayer that this guy had told me.

My wife came into the room and asked what I was doing, I said I'm praying. Now we had been practicing Catholics, so praying wasn't that unusual but usually at certain times and places. She asked what I was praying for.

I asked her to sit down, she sat on the bed.

I said Tricia something really strange has happened to me and I can't explain it.

What in the world are you talking about? she said.

I replied, I'm not quite sure myself, but I will say this, I will never touch alcohol for the rest of my life.

Stunned silence, and then, she said, what's happened?

I said I don't know.

Without going into a great deal of detail about the following dialogue, It is suffice to say that, this incident happened 24 years ago and I have not had a drink or a smoke nor have I ever been even remotely tempted to touch either. I attend the Seventh-day Adventist church every Sabbath and I am free. I found out later that this mans' name was Don Thompson, I saw him again when he came to my Baptism and I have never seen him since.

Now if you want fact. That's fact.

You think this is unusual, let me tell you something else that is totally unexplainable. My wife and I were in Scotland for a holiday. It was in March, it can get pretty cold in Scotland in March.

One day when we were touring the Isle of Arran on the west coast, we decided to visit the Cave of the King. Legend has it that Robert Bruce, King of Scotland, hid from the English in this cave. This is where the story of the spider trying to get from one side of the cave to the other came from.

To reach this cave we had to cross a golf course, go down a steep stony hill and then climb over very sharp and slippery rocks it was very desolate and deserted. Eventually we got to the cave, took some photos and started back.

It was about 3.00pm and darkness was not that far away but we weren't too concerned, we would get back before it got dark. We had gone about 100 metres when the sole of my shoe fell off. I was stuck I couldn't walk over the rocks they were cutting my foot and it was getting late. We tried to tie the shoe together but it didn't work. This was a serious problem darkness was not far away, my mobile phone was useless and it was getting very cold.

I was starting to get really stressed; I was trying to hobble on, when I noticed that my wife had stopped about five metres behind me. "What are you doing"?

I asked rather angrily.

"I'm praying" she said. We continued on for a few minutes then my wife said "John look",

"look at what", I replied

she said "look over there".

I turned and looked and I could not believe what I saw. There lying on the ground was a shoe. It was a right foot shoe and although it was surrounded by puddles, it was bone dry and it fitted me.

Can you imagine what went through my mind when I saw that shoe? I still can't and I was there. I put the shoe on and we walked back wearing one black and one blue shoe. There you go. You want proof that my God answers prayer. You've got it and you cannot take that away from me.

Just one more experience, which added to all the other experiences I have had in my life, for knowing that my God is real.

In 2001 I was 60 years of. I had lost every cent I had in a business that went bust. I was broke, I was in a state of depression and I had no idea what to do.

So I prayed and I prayed and nothing happened, at least I couldn't see anything happening.

To cut a long story short let's jump ahead to 2012. I am now 71, I am completely out of debt. I have renovated and paid off my house, I bought a brand new car and paid cash for it. I have a healthy bank balance. I have never bet on the lottery or any other form of gambling. I have never inherited any money from anywhere but during the 11 years that passed since 2001 some unbelievable things happened. My wife got a really good job as a case manager and I got work from companies that I hardly even knew existed I can honestly hang this sign on my chest. "CAREFUL GOD AT WORK"

I am in no way preaching a prosperity doctrine here, I am not suggesting for a minute that if you turn to God you will become rich and famous, the very opposite may happen, but if you genuinely trust in God, whatever He has in mind for you, you will find an amazing way of dealing with it.

When I look back on these experiences in my life, I was an alcoholic, I was naked "without a shoe", I was in a state of depression with no money. I now look at one of Gods promises in the Bible it is in Chapter 8 Verses 37–39 in the book of Romans. Just drink in what it says.

Romans 8:37–39. Yet in all these things we are more than conquerors through Him who loved us. 38 For I am persuaded that neither death nor life, nor angels nor principalities nor powers, nor things present nor things to come, 39 nor height nor depth, nor any other created thing, shall be able to separate us from the love of God which is in Christ Jesus our Lord.

I feel saddened; I really do, for those people who have never experienced the Love of God in their heart.

But please don't misinterpret that as feeling sorry for them, I don't. It's your decision, you have the free will to do whatever you like. What I am saying is that for those people who have never experienced it for whatever reason, you are missing something unique and that is what makes it sad.

I wish you would take a couple of minutes to think about it, just stop and ask yourself, "I wonder if by some remote chance I have missed something.

One of my mother in laws favorite sayings was, "You don't know what you don't know" Sometimes by just taking a few steps down an unfamiliar road you can discover wonders that you never knew existed and never thought could exist.

As I said before, at any and almost every minute of our life, we have to make decisions. The decision you are faced with now is, if you have studied all the evidence available with an open mind, and still choose to believe that evolution is scientific fact. The only reason you can possibly have for making that decision is that you want to believe it, and you have every right in the world to make that choice. You have every right in the world to choose to believe that you are nothing more than a piece of evolved dirt, a product of thousands of accidents without any purpose, any reason, or any real value. Or you can chose to believe that you are an incredibly, beautifully designed, sophisticated creation. One of the most refined pieces of machinery on the planet, made by God for a particular purpose.

But before you make that decision; just think about the fascinating process you need to employ in order to make any informed and intelligent decision.

Where did that come from?

Well, at the end of the day, does this Emperor have any clothes? The obvious answer is that not only does the Emperor have no clothes; the fact is, there is no Emperor.

GOD BLESS

John Taylor
jt4402@gmail.com